Smithsonian

THE
NATIONAL ZOO
AND CONSERVATION
BIOLOGY INSTITUTE

BY TAMRA B. ORR

CAPSTONE PRESS
a capstone imprint

Smithsonian is published by Capstone Press,
1710 Roe Crest Drive, North Mankato, Minnesota 56003
www.mycapstone.com

Library of Congress Cataloging-in-Publication Data
Library of Congress Cataloging-in-Publication data is available on the Library of Congress website.
978-1-5157-7980-3 (library binding)
978-1-5157-7990-2 (paperback)
978-1-5157-8008-3 (eBook PDF)

Editorial Credits
Michelle Hasselius, editor; Sarah Bennett, designer; Kelli Lageson, media researcher;
Laura Manthe, production specialist

Our very special thanks to Jen Zoon, Communications Specialist, Smithsonian's National Zoo and Conservation
Biology Institute, for her review. Capstone would also like to thank the following at Smithsonian Enterprises:
Kealy Gordon, Product Development Manager; Ellen Nanney, Licensing Manager; Brigid Ferraro, Vice President,
Education and Consumer Products; Carol LeBlanc, Senior Vice President, Education, and Consumer Products;
and Christopher A. Liedel, President.

Photo Credits
All photos courtesy ©2017 National Zoo and Conservation Biology Institute, Smithsonian: Tony Barthel, Jessie
Cohen, Amy Enchelmeyer, Connor Mallon, Adam Mason, Mehgan Murphy, Gil Myers, Clyde Nichimura, and Abby
Wood; except: Alamy: REUTERS/Pawan Kumar, 13 (top); Shutterstock: blackeagleEMJ, 15, CoolKengzz, cover
(design element, used throughout), David M. Schrader, 4 (design element, used throughout), Eric Patterson,
10 (right), Everett Historical, 4 (top right), Ondrej Chvatal, 23 (bottom), ppl, 8 (bottom right), Somchai Som, 8
(middle right), tea maeklong, 8 (top right)

Printed in the United States of America.
010399F17

Table of Contents

The Smithsonian's National Zoo and Conservation Biology Institute

At the Smithsonian's National Zoo in Washington, D.C., visitors are introduced to fascinating and rare animals. But the Zoo does much more than provide a place to see animals. Scientists and other staff who take care of these animals bring awareness to endangered species. Their goal is to save these animals before they disappear from the planet.

⬆ visitors to the Smithsonian's National Zoo watch a giant panda in its habitat

In 1974 the Smithsonian Conservation Biology Institute was founded in Front Royal, Virginia. At the Institute experts study these endangered animals. They learn about the animals' health, reproduction, habitats, potential diseases, and much more.

By the Numbers

National Zoo size:	Conservation Biology Institute size:	number of zoo animals:	number of animal species:
163 acres	**3,200 acres**	**1,800**	**300**

Aldabra Tortoise

What is big, slow, and lives longer than most people? It's the Aldabra tortoise! This animal is one of the largest land tortoises in the world. Male tortoises can grow up to 4 feet (1.2 meters) long and weigh 550 pounds (250 kilograms). Females are smaller. They weigh around 330 pounds (150 kg). Found on the Aldabra Island, these animals have long necks, elephant-like legs, and small, scale-covered heads.

—Fact—

The oldest Aldabra tortoise on record lived to be 255 years old.

The Zoo has three Aldabra tortoises. Two tortoises are around 80 years old. The other is 100 years old. The first tortoise arrived in 1956, and the other two arrived 20 years later. Visitors can see these animals in the Zoo's *Reptile Discovery Center*.

⬆ At the Zoo the Aldabra tortoises eat salad and hay three times a day. They can also eat cactus pads, carrots, and sweet potatoes.

Vietnamese Mossy Frog

True to its name, the Vietnamese mossy frog looks like a clump of moss. Its bumpy skin is green and black. The amphibian makes its home in Vietnam. It lives inside wet caves, along streams, under rocks, and on floating plants.

The Zoo has one Vietnamese mossy frog. **It munches on crickets,**

cockroaches,

and earthworms during the day.

At only 3.5 inches (8.8 centimeters) long, the little frog is found in the *Reptile Discovery Center*.

—Fact—
Other species of mossy frog look like tree bark and even bird poop.

Red Panda

Although this mammal is called a red panda, it's not related to the giant panda. However, both species are from Asia and eat bamboo.

The Smithsonian's National Zoo has two red pandas in the *Asia Trail* exhibit. Tusa and Asa came to the Zoo in 2015. Their habitat has an outdoor enclosure with plenty of places to climb, play, and rest. Visitors can also see the red pandas inside their habitat through a viewing window.

Endangered

Red pandas are endangered. Although legally protected in several countries, the animal's population has been reduced by half in the past 20 years. The Smithsonian's National Zoo and Conservation Biology Institute work to save these animals. More than 100 surviving cubs have been born at these places since 1962.

↑ Asa in its habitat at the Zoo

Gharial

Once you see the gharial in the Zoo's *Reptile Discovery Center*, you'll never forget what it looks like. Related to crocodiles, the gharial can grow as long as 23 feet (7 m). The reptile has a long, narrow snout. The male gharial has a bump on the end of its snout called a ghara, which makes a loud buzzing hum. This hum attracts females. The gharial's jaws are lined with sharp teeth, perfect for grabbing and holding slippery fish.

—Fact—

The reptile is known by two different names. It's called a gharial and a gavial.

⬆ The gharial is very fast in water, but it can't walk on land. It has to slide on its belly to move forward.

Did You Know?

The gharial has the largest eggs of all the crocodile species. One egg weighs around 6 ounces (160 grams).

—Fact—

The gharial is considered critically endangered. This means gharials are at a very high risk for extinction in the wild.

Goliath Bird-Eating Tarantula

At the *Amazonia* exhibit, you will see a huge female spider crawling inside a terrarium. The goliath bird-eating tarantula is the largest tarantula in the world. It's as big as a dinner plate! The spider's body can be up to 4.75 inches (12 cm) long. Its leg span is 11 inches (28 cm).

⬆ Goliath bird-eating tarantulas have eight eyes, but they can't see well. They use the hairs on their legs and abdomens to feel the vibrations in the ground.

—Fact—

The animal's fangs fold down underneath its body. The spider has to jump on top of its prey to strike.

The goliath bird-eating tarantula is found in the rainforests of northern South America. It eats birds, as well as mice, frogs, and lizards. At the Zoo the spider eats cockroaches.

Screaming Hairy Armadillo

Visitors to the *Small Mammal House* will meet two animals with big voices. Screaming hairy armadillos screech loudly to scare away predators.

The animal is one of the smallest species of hairy armadillo. It weighs 1.9 pounds (.86 kg) and is up to 15.7 inches (39.9 cm) long, not including its tail. Like other armadillos the screaming hairy armadillo is covered in overlapping armorlike scales. But it also has white and brown hair between its scales and on its belly.

—Fact—

This armadillo is found in the sandy areas of Argentina, Bolivia, and Paraguay.

Did You Know?

To catch tasty grubs and insects in the ground, the screaming hairy armadillo digs a hole. Then it turns its head in circles inside the hole to loosen its food from the dirt.

⬆ The armadillo eats plants, insects, and small animals. At the Zoo it also eats bananas and sweet potatoes.

Land Hermit Crab

The land hermit crab needs the right kind of habitat to survive. The invertebrate lives on land, but it needs to be near water to keep its gills and inside shell wet. It also needs access to shells. As the crab grows, it abandons its shell for a larger one.

At the Smithsonian these crabs make their homes in the *Think Tank* exhibit. They eat crab food along with fruits and vegetables.

Did You Know?

The land hermit crab varies in size. Some species are a fraction of an inch long, while others can grow to the size of a coconut.

← The crab uses its large left claw for balance, to protect itself, and to hold onto tree limbs. The smaller right claw is used to bring food and water to its mouth.

—Fact—

Some hermit crabs eat their old shells.

Zoo Webcams

If you'd like to see some the Zoo's animals from home, check out their webcams. They are streaming live all day, every day.

Elephant Cam

Watch the Zoo's six Asian elephants: Ambika, Shanthi, Bozie, Kamala, Swarna, and Maharani

Giant Panda Cam

Two cameras let online visitors watch three giant pandas: Tian Tian, Mei Xiang, and Bei Bei

Lion Cam

Watch African lions Luke, Naba, and Shera in their outdoor habitat. You can also see inside the lions' den when cubs are at the Zoo.

Silver Arowana

The "bony-tongued" fish can be found swimming in the Zoo's *Amazonia* exhibit. The silver arowana earned its nickname because of a bone on the bottom of its mouth. It looks like a toothy tongue. The silver arowana's mouth is on top of its body. It can open in three pieces.

When the silver arowana is hunting, it waits underwater for large insects or small birds and mammals. Then it jumps out of the water to catch its prey.

—Fact—

The silver arowana grows more than 39 inches (99 cm) long.

Did You Know?

The silver arowana changes color as it ages. Its silver scales shift to shades of red, blue, and green.

Abyssinian Ground Hornbill

You might think you've stepped back in time when you spot the Abyssinian ground hornbill. With its large beak and bony casque, the bird looks like it could have roamed with the dinosaurs.

—Fact—

Sometimes male and female hornbills sing together.

The hornbill has a colorful neck, long legs, and bright facial markings. It can grow about 40 inches (102 cm) tall and weigh as much as 11 pounds (5 kg). The Zoo has a male Abyssinian ground hornbill named Karl. Its habitat is in the *Cheetah Conservation Station*.

Did You Know?

The hornbill has some of the longest eyelashes in nature. The eyelashes are made of feathers and help protect the animal's eyes from dust and debris.

Arapaima

The arapaima is one of the largest freshwater fish in the world. It can grow up to 10 feet (3 m) long and weigh up to 440 pounds (199.6 kg). Unlike other freshwater fish, the arapaima breathes air. The fish can survive for 24 hours on land and stay underwater for up to 20 minutes. It is found in Brazil, Peru, and Guyana. The Zoo's arapaima live in the *Amazonia* exhibit.

⬆ The fish's mouth is like a vacuum. It can suck up fruits, seeds, insects, birds, and other fish nearby.

—Fact—

The arapaima can easily shred prey with its sharp teeth. It even has teeth on the roof of its mouth.

Japanese Giant Salamander

Visit the Zoo's *Reptile Discovery Center,* and you'll find the Japanese giant salamander. The amphibian is the second largest salamander species in the world. It can grow up to 5 feet (1.5 m) long. It is found in streams on the Japanese islands of Honshu, Kyushu, and Shikoku.

← This amphibian usually stays underwater, but it can survive above water as long as its skin stays moist.

Nicknamed the "big pepper fish," the animal protects itself from predators by secreting sticky, toxic ooze that smells like Japanese peppers. The Japanese giant salamander can't see well, so it uses its senses of smell and touch to find food. These salamanders eat turtles, snakes, and small mammals.

—Fact—

A Japanese giant salamander lived for 52 years at the Amsterdam Zoo.

Double-Wattled Cassowary

The double-wattled cassowary is a tall, flightless bird that is related to ostriches and emus. The bird is 6 feet (1.8 m) tall and has a large, bony casque on its head. It also has a razor sharp, 5-inch (13-cm) claw on each foot. The double-wattled cassowary is considered one of the most dangerous birds in the world. The bird hisses, jumps in the air, and kicks its feet if it feels threatened.

Did You Know?

The double-wattled cassowary is found in the tropical rainforests of Australia and Papua New Guinea. Only 1,500 of these birds live in their natural habitat.

⬇ Male cassowaries build nests and sit on their eggs. After the eggs hatch, males take care of the chicks for up to nine months.

The Zoo has had one cassowary. Earline left the Smithsonian National Zoo in 2017. The Zoo hopes to get another cassowary when the *Experience Migration* exhibit opens in 2020.

—Fact—

The bird is also known as the southern cassowary.

Glossary

amphibian (am-FIB-ee-uhn)—a cold-blooded animal with a backbone; amphibians live in water when young and can live on land as adults

casque (KASK)—a bony growth on an animal's head that looks like a helmet

enclosure (en-KLOH-zhur)—an area closed in by a fence or wall

endangered (en-DAYN-jurd)—at risk of dying out

extinction (ek-STINGKT-shun)—no longer living; an extinct animal is one that has died out, with no more of its kind

gill (GIL)—a body part on the side of fish and some insects to breathe underwater

invertebrate (in-VUR-tuh-brit)—an animal without a backbone

mammal (MAM-uhl)—a warm-blooded animal that breathes air; mammals have hair or fur

moss (MOSS)—a soft, clumpy plant that usually grows in swamps and wetlands

predator (PRED-uh-tur)—an animal that hunts other animals for food

reptile (REP-tile)—a cold-blooded animal that breathes air and has a backbone; most reptiles lay eggs and have scaly skin

snout (SNOUT)—the long, front part of an animal's head; the snout includes the nose, mouth, and jaws

species (SPEE-seez)—a group of plants or animals that share common characteristics

wattle (WOT-uhl)—a fleshy part of skin that hangs under the necks of certain birds

Read More

Baxter, Bethany. *Caimans, Gharials, Alligators, and Crocodiles.* Awesome Armored Animals. New York: PowerKids Press, 2014.

Gregory, Josh. *Red Pandas.* Nature's Children. New York: Children's Press, 2017.

Rake, Matthew. *Creatures of the Rain Forest.* Real-Life Monsters. Minneapolis: Lerner Publications, 2016.

Critical Thinking Questions

1. The gharial is considered critically endangered. What does it mean when a species is critically endangered?

2. How does the screaming hairy armadillo catch grubs and insects in the ground?

3. Why is the Japanese giant salamander called the "big pepper fish"?

Internet Sites

Use FactHound to find Internet sites related to this book.

Visit *www.facthound.com*

Just type in 9781515779803 and go.

Check out projects, games and lots more at
www.capstonekids.com

Index